PEARL MOTHER

~a Woman without Children~

Unnur Arndísardóttir

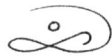

Copyright © 2023 Unnur Arndísardóttir

Pearl Mother
by: © Unnur Arndísardóttir, 2023
Cover design & illustrations: © Heather Wulfers
English translation: Kelsey Hopkins

All rights reserved. No part of this book may be reproduced without written permission from the publisher/author, except by a reviewer who may quote brief passages or reproduce illustrations in a review with appropriate credits; nor may any part of this book be reproduced, stored in a retrieval system, or transmitted in any form or by any means - electronic, mechanical, photocopying, recording, or other - without written permission from the publisher/author.

The information in this book is true and complete to the best of our knowledge. All recommendations are made without guarantee on the part of the publisher/author. The publisher/author disclaims any liability in connection with the use of this information.

I dedicate this book to my mother Arndis Sveina, and to all my For-Mothers.

The Pearl Mother, the daughter, holding our lineage sacred.

Mother of pearl is the shell that provides space for creation. She influences her surroundings and leaves behind colour on the pearl itself.

Women without children are Pearl Mothers. We possess all the characteristics and strength of the Mother, but we do not create children. Our "children" – our pearls – appear in the form of our works of art, our labours of love, and everything we nourish and bring to life.

We Pearl Mothers offer the world our rainbows and our magic. We nourish, give life, and create — just not in the form of a baby.

1. The Beginning

This began before I was born – it was written in the stars. Mom described how I woke up one morning when I was four years old and announced that I would never have kids when I grew up. This took my mother by surprise. I was very perceptive as a child and have had the gift of second sight since birth, and many things came to me clearly in dreams. When I was growing up I had my dolls and I enjoyed playing house — but I always found it strange whenever my friends started talking about what they were going to name their kids and how many they planned on having. I never gave this any thought, I was never caught up in the idea of becoming a mother at some point in the future. That sentiment only came to me when I was around twenty, and I had a boyfriend who longed to have children. We talked about having kids and what they would look like, and only then did I feel a certain yearning in my belly – the yearning for children. Then when I met my husband years later, my life began to revolve around becoming a mom, and *only* becoming a mom. I made a list of names and I did everything within my power to try to conceive.

You see, I had appendicitis when I was fourteen years old. My appendix had ruptured and I'd gone for two days with it ruptured inside my body. There hadn't been much pain, but I did have a high fever, and when it refused to come down, my mom started to worry. She took me to the doctor, who thought I had a uterine inflammation and sent me to the gynecology department for a laparoscopy. The procedure revealed that my appendix had ruptured all over the place. I was cut open and all the pus removed. Or so we thought. My high fever persisted, and it eventually came to light that my abdomen hadn't been cleaned out well enough. I was put on strong medication for several weeks in order to get it all out of me. Four years later, I came down with a massive uterine inflammation and was admitted to where I went for my second laparoscopy. There I find out that my Fallopian tubes are extremely inflamed. After the examination, the doctor informs me that there's a 50/50 chance after such a severe infection that my Fallopian tubes will fuse together, and will therefore be unable to carry eggs down into the uterus. As a result, I'd most likely need help conceiving in the future. I was eighteen years old at the time and not thinking about having kids — in fact, I didn't want to have kids at all. But I was touched by how my dear mother reacted to the news with tears and a deep embrace. It was then that I realised that this was most likely going to impact my life in the future.

I met my husband when I was around thirty. We were head over heels in love, and we fantasised about having a baby together. We tried and tried for a whole year before finally deciding to seek help. Our IVF process lasted for six years — we tried our best, but nothing worked. During our final embryo transfer procedure at Art Medica in Iceland, the doctor let slip that he thought I'd have to have my Fallopian tubes removed. They were always swelling, filling with liquid, and causing me pain. Ever since I was young. The doctor said he thought the Fallopian tubes were probably interfering with our poor embryos, preventing them from implanting in the uterus, and that's why none of them survived. Thinking back, I'm hurt by and disappointed in the doctors back home for failing to examine me well enough to discover everything that would await me down the road.

My husband and I decided to stop trying. To stop wasting all our energy and money in these fertility treatments. To stop trying for kids and start taking care of our own lives and our own happiness. To embrace a child-free lifestyle and start enjoying ourselves. We moved to Copenhagen, where my husband was studying, and began making our dreams come true. I decided to go to a gynecologist there for advice about my Fallopian tubes, which continued causing me pain, pressure, and discomfort. During our first interview, she recommended that I have them removed, and expressed shock at the fact that the doctors back home in Iceland hadn't sent me for such a procedure long before. She told me that now I just deserved to be pain-free and to feel good — for my own sake. I teared up at the mere thought that maybe I could live a life without pain, and that maybe I deserved to after 22 years of suffering.

On July 18, 2018, I went into surgery in Copenhagen. This was supposed to be a minor operation, and I was supposed to go home two hours afterwards. But the procedure proved to be much more difficult than expected. After my ruptured appendix and all the uterine inflammations over the years, scar tissue had formed around all my abdominal organs. The doctors could hardly discern one organ from another during the operation, so they had to call in a specialist to cut away the scar tissue and separate them. My uterus and Fallopian tubes were stuck to my intestines and stomach wall, and the Fallopian tubes were weary and withered after all the inflammation over such a long time — they were stuck fast behind the uterus, swollen and filled with fluid. The doctors managed to remove two-thirds of the Fallopian tubes on either side. The fimbriae were so stuck and hidden so far behind the uterus that the doctors weren't able to get them out, and didn't want to take the risk. But the part that was always becoming inflamed was finally gone. The doctor told me after the surgery that this was the reason I couldn't conceive naturally in the first place, and that none of the fertility treatments I'd been through had worked because the environment in my uterus wasn't conducive to the implantation of the embryo. On the other hand, my uterus finally had some peace and quiet and could hang freely in my abdomen, no longer wrapped up in scar tissue and attached to other organs.

All the doctors and nurses who took care of me that day were women. In humility and gratitude, I'd arrived at the heart of the matter at the age of 40. I had finally experienced the sacrifice of my Fallopian tubes and gained the inner peace I had yearned for in recent years. You see, I always believed that having my own child would bring me the peace that I so longed for. But somehow, the almighty Goddess herself had brought me that peace in the initiation that this operation was in my life.

My path towards reconciliation

While I was going through the process of trying to conceive, I felt so alone. No matter where I looked, it was so hard to find any kind of material or writing on infertility and self-empowerment after unsuccessful fertility treatments. There are endless self-help books and courses for all the women of the world, but almost nothing for those of us who can't have children. It's as if the subject is completely taboo, and we're so fragile we don't even want to talk about it. After looking into it more closely, I found out that research says that one out of every six women struggles with infertility. Research also says that less than 30% of IVF/in vitro fertilization procedures are successful. This made me think of all of the other women dealing with the same thing as I'm dealing with, and just the thought of not being alone brought me a little more peace. Not only that, it also sparked the desire to reach out to those women who carry the same wound that I do.

Throughout my process, I've compiled the things that have worked for me. I say worked for me — though as infertile women, we know we may never fully come to terms with our infertility. These are just the things that helped me along my own path.

We carry this sorrow inside of us always. But I choose to regard it as a wound that I did my best to cleanse and heal. The scar is always there, but it has stopped stinging, irritating me and controlling my well-being. What helped me the most during my process was never quitting, never giving up on my body. Through exercise, yoga, breathing and meditation, and regular relaxation, I was able to connect more closely with my body and my life. I often felt angry at my body and at odds with the Goddess and life itself. But something always kept me on track. I think it must have been this longing to live. To experience life — even though it can be difficult at times.

I found that I was also in constant communion with nature and the Goddess. Constantly asking and inquiring about the subject at hand. Constantly listening for signs and clues about having kids and the spiritual side of trying to conceive. Constantly trying to reach a conclusion and find contentment. My communion with nature has been in the form of walking in nature and outdoor ceremonies. I love creating ceremonies and devotions to the Goddess and to myself. My conversation with the Goddess during this process has allowed me to realise that this project of mine is in constant flow — as it by fate. Wherever I've traveled during this process, I've visited churches, chapels, temples, and sacred places to pray and connect with the moment. I've lost count of all the candles I've lit, praying for a miracle. As my life progresses, I realise what a great gift it's been in my life to be able to experience this grief, sorrow, anger, and discontentment. To be able to go through all of this and still find hope and the desire for life. To realise that life goes on, and that somehow I've always met the right people at the right time.

On a concert tour around Europe, my husband Jón Tryggvi and I had the good fortune of meeting a couple struggling with the same difficulties as us — they couldn't have children. The man had organized our concert, and he and his wife had invited us for dinner and to stay in their living room. We cooked together and enjoyed each other's company over a wonderful evening. As the evening drew on, this topic of conversation came up. We shared the same wound of being unable to conceive. Towards the end of the night, we women talked in private and from the heart about these issues. The feeling of being unable to have children, and what little understanding society seemed to have of the problem. We both worked in healing, and she said that more and more pregnant women were coming to her for treatment, just as if the universe – God or the Goddess – were giving her the chance to heal her own troubles or problem. It was difficult and painful for her, but she said she'd never give up — ever.

That evening together had a profound impact on my life and my entire conception journey. For the first time, I felt the importance of discussing these issues with someone who understood me completely. I'd discovered that it didn't matter how much my friends, my mother, and the women around me tried to understand my problem, it was a nearly impossible feat for them to fully understand all my sorrow because they'd never experienced the same. A woman who has children cannot fully understand the grief of a woman who can't conceive. She can imagine what it must be like, but never properly understand. Even though I had the best friends and mother in the world, who wanted to do everything for me and who showed me the utmost sympathy and love, there was always something missing. This problem was solved when I finally had the opportunity to talk with another woman who fully understood how I felt. That woman and I formed a strong bond that evening, and I'm eternally grateful to have experienced myself the importance of discussing these things with another woman — one who understands me. To feel the sisterhood among women who have endured this great sorrow.

It's in our own hands to bless ourselves.

We have spent too much time waiting for someone else to come and break the spell that's holding us down, or to heal us and come to our rescue. Now I place this in your hands. Now I give you the gift that was so precious to me, the gift of discovering that I can heal myself.

I wish you a sacred journey, dear sister.

2. Pearl Mother

Even if a woman can't have children, she still carries Mother energy and Mother love within her. With this energy, we continue to nourish our surroundings, our friends and family, our work and our art.

I had a hard time adopting the word "infertile" and using it about myself. You see, I don't think I'm an infertile person. I compose music, Goddess ceremonies and meditations, and I take on all kinds of projects in my life and in my work — all things that require creative energy and perseverance. "Infertile" in the truest sense of the word doesn't describe me at all, I don't think. I carried this with me for quite some time. If I'm not infertile, then what am I? I felt like some other word for this was missing. Then one morning, between sleep and awake, one came to me: Pearl Mother. Yes, I am a Pearl Mother!

As a Pearl Mother, I can be proud. I am proud to be a mother of pearls, mother to my art, my music, and all my other works. I can be proud of all the pearls that flow from me. I always felt that being "infertile" carried a negative energy. But being a Pearl Mother brings positivity, strength, courage, and power that only a Pearl Mother can have. I consider being a Pearl Mother — being unable to have children or choosing not to — a magic power. We women who carry this energy possess a kind of supernatural inner strength, and we occupy a unique position.

It's nothing new on Mother Earth that some people don't have children. Pearl Mothers and Fathers have always existed in our community. They're just people who for some reason don't have children. It's not something to be regarded only with sorrow or pity. We Pearl Mothers and Fathers just have a different role to fill, and it's no less important. The space and breathing room that we have — those of use whose time and energy don't go into raising children — provide an opportunity for a different kind of life and work. We can apply ourselves differently in our community. We have the option of a different kind of life. We have a different kind of energy and time that creates the potential for great inner strength and spiritual power. I believe that being a Pearl Mother is my "superpower".

I've always enjoyed thinking of my music and my works as my children. A lot of work goes into releasing a song. I've put loving care into composing the music and the lyrics, I've arranged the song and prepared it for the world, I've practiced it many times. Then the recording process begins, which is time-consuming work. And then it has to be mixed. Once the song is ready, marketing takes over — photography and even videography, so that the song sounds nice to others. This is a long process and it can be difficult, but it's also beautiful and tender.

I've noticed in my collaborations with other artists, for example, that we women place a different emphasis on our works than men. I've done a lot of work with men in music — and I admire them for being able to compose a song, practice it for one night, and play it at a concert the next day. It's as if men have a different kind of courage than we women. They create — and immediately release their creation for the eyes of the universe to behold. I always need to carry the song with me for a long time before I feel like it's ready to flow out into the world, and I've often scolded myself for being too much of a perfectionist. But I had a sort of inner epiphany when I realised that masculine energy and feminine work differently in the creative process.

If we look only at the world's fundamental creative energy, men shoot forth seed. We can consider a man's seed his creation. Perhaps they aren't very concerned about whether their seed becomes fertilized, whether it survives, where it lands. It's in a man's nature to release it — and often. Women, on the other hand, only have one egg per month that's capable of being fertilized, and if it is, a woman carries a child for nine months before it's ready to see the light of day.

When I began to reflect on my artistic process, I saw a comparison here. I want to nurture what I create — I carry it inside me for nine months until the work is complete and ready to see the light of day. I have to feel good about what I create. And then once I'm ready to bring my children into the world, I look at these gifts and my works as pearls. I am a Pearl Mother, gathering pearls and stringing them into a beautiful pearl necklace that I am so proud to wear.

It's of great help to me to channel my energy into something positive. It's one thing to turn your life around and come to terms with infertility. But to be proud of it is a completely different matter — and I believe only very few of us will ever arrive at that place, and some perhaps never will. But I choose to embrace its positive qualities. Being a Pearl Mother is important work. It is essential that each and every person here on this earth creates works of art and sets them free. I believe that each and every person has a purpose, that we aren't here by coincidence, but instead to do good things.

What pearls are you collecting?
What pearls are you giving into the world?

Looking at myself as a Pearl Mother rather than infertile has transformed my life for the better. Now I look forward to nurturing the projects that I undertake, and gathering them onto my string of pearls.

3. I breathe

Breathing and breathing exercises are one of the things that have given me the most in life. Regular deep breathing has provided profound peace and tranquility, and the much-needed space and serenity that have brought me contentment and healing.

Yogic studies teach the importance of breathing, and that this is in fact the first step in the entire healing process. The first thing we do when we're born into this world and this life is inhale deeply. When we transition from sickness into healing and good health, breathing is indeed the first step. I always recommend breathing and breathing exercises on your journey towards a better life.

At any stage of the conception process, whether during IVF treatments or after deciding to stop trying for kids, I absolutely recommend the gift of regular deep breathing.

Breathing is vital to us humans. Yoga teaches various breathing exercises both to help bring oxygen into our body, blood, and organs, and also to revive our bodies' life energy.

We humans can't live without oxygen or go very long without breathing, yet most of us are unaware of just how shallow we breathe in our day-to-day lives. When babies are born, it's often said that they breathe perfectly. Infants breathe deep into their lungs, then as they get older it's as if their breathing grows shorter, and as adults we only take in a very small amount of oxygen into our lungs. Deep breathing has often been considered a way to prevent disease and to bring our bodies towards wellness and improved health.

Breathing helps us arrive at the present moment, it helps us find peace and love within ourselves. Deep breathing soothes the body and soul, and gives us the peace and serenity needed to achieve perfect harmony with our own body and with our life.

Breathing exercises boost our energy, reduce stress, improve memory, and increase concentration.

Breathing is a wonderful way to better connect with ourselves. Our health improves and we get an even greater sense of calm, ease, and well-being out of life. Breathing deeply for only ten minutes a day can make all the difference in your life.

When you first start, it's good to begin just by practicing breathing deeply. Get into a comfortable sitting position, either lotus position on the ground, or in a chair with the soles of your feet on the floor. Close your eyes and check your breathing. Is it typically deep or shallow? Fast or slow? Just pay attention to how you breathe, without judging it in any way. Then start gradually deepening your breath. Breathe deep into your belly, then slowly exhale. This will be quite enough to begin with. And remember, it's fine no matter how you breathe, but it's always possible to improve. It's good to gradually incorporate breathing exercises into your daily life — just ten minutes a day can transform your life for the better.

Ujjayi – Ocean breath

Get into a comfortable position with your back straight. You can do this exercise in lotus position or in a chair with the soles of your feet flat on the ground.

Slowly turn your attention to your breath. Slowly inhale, slowly exhale. Then contract your throat a little so that you make a "hsss" sound. This sound doesn't have to be loud, just loud enough to hear it gently. This is sound of the ocean. We inhale slowly, then calmly exhale. Lengthen your breaths and breathe as deeply as you can. You can hold your breath slightly after both the inhale and the exhale, but be careful not to hold your breath for too long if you have high blood pressure.

Ocean breath calms the waves within us — waves of emotion, waves of thought, waves of stress. I like to imagine my inner sea going mirror-smooth.

Heart-centered breathing
~ Heart Mudra ~

A mudra is a hand position. For example, when we hold our hands a certain way while we breathe deeply. The heart mudra connects the consciousness with the heart and brings tenderness, strength, and warmth into our emotional life. It is especially effective if you sit with your hands in the heart position after yoga or meditation.

Allow yourself to sit with your hands over your chest in the heart mudra for 3-5 minutes. Take a deep breath and let yourself feel peace and tranquility spread over your heart and soul.

4. I feel

Yoga, breathing, and relaxation are among the things that have enriched my life the most. During my conception journey and after I decided to stop trying, yoga brought me the serenity that I needed to take on this project in the first place, to dare to get to know myself better, and even to honour myself throughout this whole process. There are many types of yoga, and I encourage you to find the one that suits you. I've learned several different kinds of yoga over the years, and I'd like to share some of the exercises that have helped me the most along my journey. The exercises I share here I learned from my Yoga Teacher training with Ateeka, that she called Restorative Yoga Somatics. Where we learned to dedicate to unique sensitivity, listening and very gentle movement in each pose. The training with Ateeka helped me extremely on my healing journey with yoga, and has affected the way I listen to my body now.
I offer you to try these out, and then find what is best for you.

Supported Child's Pose

~Salamba Balasana~

Child's Pose has a calming effect on the nervous system. This pose helps you ground yourself and promotes well-being and harmony within your own body. Here you can completely surrender to the support of your cushion and the ground beneath you. This exercise brings you deep peace, profound calm and a sense of security. It calms the stomach and abdomen, helps ease tension and relieve pain in the womb and relaxes the lower back and hips.

- The exercise –

- Keep your knees wide enough apart that your stomach has plenty of room to completely relax between your legs. It's good to have a body pillow or other big, long cushion under you during this exercise. Allow your chest and head to rest on the cushion. Use as many cushions and blankets as you need to attain a comfortable position. Begin with one cheek resting against the cushion, then switch to the other cheek halfway through the exercise. Hold this position for 3-5 minutes.

- If you experience knee pain in this position, try sitting on the pillow and then leaning forward.

- If you feel pain in your shins or ankles in this position, try placing a rolled-up blanket under each ankle

Supported Angel Pose

The Angel Pose calms and creates space in the hips and pelvic region, relaxes and soothes the lumbar area, and creates an opening in the area of the heart. This pose helps with relaxation and calm. Throughout the conception process and in times of stress on the body and soul, it can be beneficial to release physical tension by practicing this pose for several minutes

- The exercise –

It's up to you how many cushions and how much support you need to relax in this position. You'll need at least one body pillow or another long cushion for your spine. You can also prop up the body pillow or cushion with at least two yoga blocks, or even another cushion and a few blankets. Place a rolled-up blanket under your knees. It can be nice to spread a blanket over yourself while lying in this position. Hold the position for 2-5 minutes.

- Note that you can also lie with your legs straight if the strain on the hips and knees is too much. You can even bend your legs with the soles of your feet on the floor.

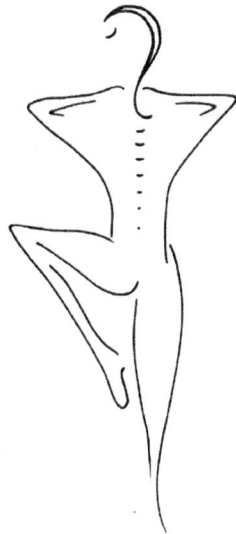

Lizard enjoying the sun
~Pratisuryasana~

Lizard Pose increases the flow of blood and oxygen to the womb and into the hips, eases premenstrual stress and menstrual pain. This pose rejuvenates the body after a long time in the same position, such as after prolonged sitting.

- The exercise –

Rest face down on your stomach with one knee bent. Place a cushion under your bent knee. The size of the cushion you use depends entirely on your body and where you feel most calm. A lot of people like to let their ankle dangle off the edge of the cushion. Support your head with a blanket or make a small "pillow" with your hands. Let yourself lie in this position and enjoy letting go completely.

Breathe deep into your belly and feel your shoulders and chest relax. Hold this position for 3-5 minutes on each side.

- Make sure that the cushion or support you use is the right size for your body. If you feel tension in your hips or lower back, you can shift your weight towards the other side or onto the leg that's extended while you hold the position. It may be helpful to have a thin cushion or blanket under your head. Try to find as comfortable a position as possible.

Root Chakra- healing touch

This touch brings healing and blessing to the vagina and the lowest chakra. It's often hard to forgive our bodies and reconcile with them after a long time trying to conceive. This hand position connects you with the root chakra and brings calm and tranquility into your life and your body.

- The exercise –

Start by rubbing your palms together to generate warmth. Place your right palm over your vagina and the left on your abdomen. Breathe deeply into your belly, and imagine that you're sending your vagina warmth, peace, and contentment every time you inhale. It's a good idea to hold this position for 1-3 minutes and enjoy breathing deeply. This is a good pose on which to end a yoga session. You may also recite kind words in your mind while you sit here and breathe: "I bring my vagina peace and healing." "I am content in my own body." "I forgive myself."

5. I let go

I felt like something happened in my body when I discovered that I couldn't have children. I'd somehow always suspected that I couldn't, but something within me transformed when my fears were confirmed. Feelings of negativity towards my body began brewing, and they had a real effect on my physical well-being.

As a yoga teacher, I spend a lot of time and energy listening to my body. My job is to teach people to love being in a body, to love breathing, to love being alive. Throughout my entire journey, I never stopped teaching yoga. I showed up for every lesson and stood before rooms full of people searching for inner peace and a deeper connection with their life and their body. There were times when I was drenched in sweat and puffy from the hormone injections I'd taken to prepare for my next round of IVF. There were times when I could hardly catch my breath for malaise and lethargy. There were times when tears streamed down my cheeks as my students lay in relaxation after a good yoga session. I never showed anybody the hell I was going through. I continued talking to my students about finding the flow and trusting it, to love their body no matter what, that the body is perfect in its imperfection. This proved to be very difficult for me — but still so infinitely rewarding. I embraced the problem and didn't let go. It would have been so easy to avoid it and forget about it. But this taught me the importance of how I think about my body. It's important that I change my mindset from feeling like there's something wrong with me to embracing my situation as a possible opportunity. It may sound cliché, but I believe that one of the most important steps in my self-healing process has been to forgive and reconcile with my body.

-Can I somehow come to terms with my body as it is?

-Can I forgive my body for being unable to bear children?

-Can I forgive myself and my role in this process?

This, I've found, has been one of the hardest things about all of this. For one thing, I'd struggled to love my body the way it is since I was a teenager, then this entered the equation. I regard it as the modern woman's most important task — to sit with our truth and learn to love our body just the way it is.

The pain of being a Pearl Mother gives us so much. The wound is ever present, but as I've said before, it eventually stops stinging and chafing. The scar remains, but it's the act of forgiveness that helps us reconcile and take pride in the wound itself. Because all the hardship we've endured gives us wisdom, knowledge, and strength. Because being a Pearl Mother is something to be proud of.

I have walked through a dark valley, I know the emotions, I know the difficulties and hardships, I forgive myself and I rise up to the future with courage, vitality, and pride, knowing that I've survived.

Love List

I recommend starting by making a list of everything that's good and beautiful about you and your abilities. This is a good first step. You may even want your partner or friends to help you with this — our friends are truly the most beautiful mirror we could ever hope for. They often see so much in us that we, for whatever reason, are unable to. Do you have a trusted confidant who can help you create your Love List?

It's also good to find compassion for yourself, to realise that you've already put so much into becoming the person you are today, and to understand how strong you already are. If you have a hard time feeling your strength in the moment, try making a list of all the effort you've made in trying to conceive. Include in your list all the time you've spent on visits to the doctor, all the treatments, and all the sleepless nights that you've carried your sorrow in silence. Then say that you haven't really put much effort into all this, and recognize that it hasn't broken you down completely. Just the fact that you're reading this shows that there's hope in your heart, a hope that's often stronger than everything else.

Maybe we'll never fully come to terms with our lot in life to never have children. But okay, we understand that this is a great wound in our life, and just the act of accepting that it will always be there is the first step towards finding forgiveness and reconciliation. We take just one step at a time, one day of reconciliation at a time, one hug at a time, one tear at a time — and finally, one smile at a time.

Meditation for Forgiveness

"I forgive you, Body — I love you just the way you are"

It can be of great benefit to keep this phrase in mind. I suggest making a habit of sitting in meditation and reciting it to yourself. Embrace these words, even if at first you don't completely agree or you don't see the truth in them. This is just one of our many steps toward reconciliation and changing our way of thinking. Just saying this to yourself regularly can have a transformative power. Try it anyway, it can't hurt!

A gift to yourself

At so many moments along my conception journey, I felt like I'd climbed the highest mountains and stood up to the greatest challenges. Typically, when people make it up Mt. Everest or graduate from challenging studies, they throw a party. I often wanted to celebrate the milestones along this journey that felt like an eternity. But when the goal is ultimately never reached, all the great strides that are achieved are overshadowed by the sorrow. My husband and I never celebrated because our wish never came true.

I believe there's a healing power to patting yourself on the back and treating yourself to something nice as a reminder of your strength and perseverance throughout everything taken upon yourself so far. Buy yourself a piece of jewelry or something you can wear that reminds you of your strength, perseverance, and courage. That way, whenever you're feeling down or having a hard time remembering and appreciating your strength and your positive qualities, you can wear this item with pride. This is one way to remind yourself regularly of what you have and that you don't give up even in the face of adversity.

A letter to the child who never was

One of the hardest, most beautiful things I've experienced in my childlessness was saying goodbye to the idea and the image of my child who never was. My life underwent a huge transformation when I finally sat down and decided to write a letter to my baby. A letter to say goodbye, in peace and love. I felt that picture in my mind of this child weighing on me, I had a hard time letting go. I'd painted such a gorgeous picture in my mind of this child who I held so close to my heart. This child, who I'd spent years trying to hold in my arms, but who was never meant to be. Just this image alone held me under a spell, I felt. One morning as I was trying to meditate, I felt driven to write my baby a final farewell. The simple act of writing this letter set off a healing process that helped me immeasurably, to finally say goodbye and cry out all my tears. I still cry when I read this letter, and that alone has brought me limitless healing. Because after all, tears possess healing power.

I encourage you to try. I know that merely mentioning this here might trigger anger and sorrow.

But this is one of the things that's helped me the most, while at the same time one of the hardest things I have ever done.

This letter was the inspiration for this book, and the beginning of my journey as a Pearl Mother.

Letter to an angel

My beloved girl, my precious angel who never arrived. I've thought so often about writing you a letter, even singing to you. But at the end of the day, I have nothing to say. Now, though, I feel like breaking the silence...

Dear love of my heart, even though you never came to me in this life, I've always held a hopeful image of you. I know you'd have resembled your dad in so many ways. I know that you'd have gotten his blue eyes and my blonde curls, and I know that we'd have danced, laughed, and sung our way through life together. I know that happiness would have surrounded our little family.

But now I'm ready to let you go. I give you permission to leave. Know that you will always have a place in my heart, and that I will always remember you. But in order for us to make peace with our life and live it to the fullest, I'm letting you go. I'm setting you free — may you be united with the Great Mother. May the Goddess bless you, hold you close, and protect you.

I ask you to let go of me, too. Because I always believed that you called upon me and that you needed me. You wanted to come to us and I heard you.

But now, so that I may have a second chance at loving life, please let me go too. Know that I will always live in your heart and I will be with you always. We will be reunited in the embrace of the Sacred Mother, in endless peace and harmony. We'll meet again there.

I will always love you, Mom

Family and friends

Throughout this whole process, I realised that it wasn't only hard for me and my husband, but also for the people around us. We often had to answer questions about why we didn't have kids. Most of the time, the most uncomfortable questions came from people who didn't know us very well, for example, people we'd run into at parties or on the street who we hadn't seen in a long time. It was as if our people — our family and closest friends — sensed what was going on, and only very few of the people who care about us the most even brought it up.

This was a good thing in many ways, but in others it was also extremely difficult. When we first embarked on this journey, we made the decision not to mention it to just anybody. We wanted keep the energy around our journey pure and to ourselves. It was hard to imagine everyone wanting to know what we were going through, and maybe feeling sorry for us. When I say 'keep the energy pure', I mean that I thought if everyone, or too many, thought of our childlessness as a problem, then maybe that problem would grow. I believe that our thinking affects our life, so the idea was to keep everything pure and clear. But of course, there remained the fact that it wasn't at all easy for us to talk about these things with just anyone. I cried a lot throughout the process itself. Tears, pain, resentment, and even anger were never far away whenever I mentioned it to my family. Thus, I simply did not want to discuss it at all with anyone.

As time went on, especially after my husband and I made the decision to stop trying and to remain child-free forever, we found it much easier to talk about.

We decided not to tell everybody at the time, and I don't regret it, especially not in retrospect. I've also heard of people who did decide to tell everybody they knew, and regretted it so much after increasingly more rounds of treatment. It proved exceptionally hard for these couples to let people know how things were going, and when they weren't going well, it made things that much worse.

I recommend being especially kind to yourself along this journey, and in my case, it was important that I not discuss it with others. I know that in many ways this was hard for the people in my life. Occasionally our interactions became awkward, and we often experienced a great sense of rejection from people when everyone pretended that everything was perfectly fine. Because the truth was that we were going through the most difficult time in our lives. This was all an extremely touchy, delicate situation.

Is it a good idea to discuss matters, to tell everyone you know? Or is it better to keep things to yourself?

But that's just the way it goes — when we're dealing with such a huge issue, we don't bring it up with just anybody, and certainly not just at any opportunity that presents itself.

It always amazes me how many people act like it's totally normal to ask just anyone why they don't have kids. Having kids seems like such a given in our society that people often develop a kind of unawareness, as if everyone has the right to just inquire about people's personal circumstances like that.

-An important point for everyone who hasn't experienced infertility: do not ask a woman why she doesn't have kids.

I've come home in tears from parties, coffee dates, trips to the grocery store, etc. thanks to inconsiderate questions from others about having kids. If a woman chooses not to have children for whatever reason, she will tell you on her own terms when the time is right — don't force an answer when it's not.

Take your time — and this could absolutely mean keeping things to yourself forever! You have the right to choose this for your own sake. You shouldn't have to deal with pressure from society, family, and friends. Choose for yourself what's right for you and your life.

6. I relax

What is relaxation?

Relaxation is when we let go of tension and stress of the daily hustle and bustle, and allow ourselves to let go. Relaxation brings rest, inner peace and calm. True relaxation happens when our body achieves perfect rest. It's a well-known fact that in today's world, fewer and fewer of us get adequate rest when we sleep, and so relaxation has gained increasing popularity. Many different instructors teach various methods of relaxation.

Yoga teaches methods of relaxation, which are said to provide the body with the restorative rest it doesn't get through sleep. Scientists today have proven the benefits of relaxation on the body, and more and more doctors in the Western world have begun prescribing relaxation.

In our fast-paced society, it can be hard to find the time to relax. In fact, finding the time is one of the greatest obstacles we encounter when we want to begin a self-nourishment routine, and it should be the first step. A relaxation session doesn't need to take long. I encourage you to start off slowly. Maybe it's enough to set the goal of relaxing for only a few minutes a day, or even just once a week when you first start. You can always increase your sessions as you go. Because that's just how it is — when we get a taste of something, we want more. Start small and then gradually take things up a notch.

I love relaxing after a walk or a good yoga session. Whenever I've exerted my body at all, I allow myself to lie down and relax for 5-10 minutes. You may also wish to set aside a few minutes for relaxation as soon as you get home from work.

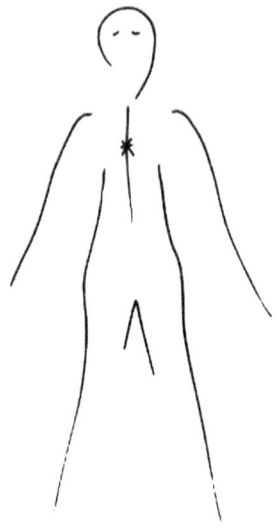

Corpse Pose
~Savasana~

This pose has a calming, rejuvenating effect on the entire body. Corpse Pose is often said to be one of the most important poses in yoga due to the importance of rest and relaxation in letting our body recharge. I will tell you here and now and I stand by it — if there's no time in your life for yoga or other such exercises, I at least recommend relaxing in Corpse Pose for 3-5 minutes every day. This pose offers the most benefit, as it provides the body with the peace and tranquility that's so needed to combat the stress of the daily grind.

All bodies are different, so you'll have to figure out what's best for you. You should be as comfortable as possible in Corpse Pose. You will want to try to position yourself so that nothing restricts you or causes discomfort.

1. Dress in comfortable clothing — warm, soft, and preferably loose and non-restrictive. It's a good idea to wear warm socks.

2. Make yourself comfortable — lie down on something soft, like a yoga mat or a blanket. If you choose to use one, place a thin cushion under your head, though it is actually better to keep your neck straight. Some people like to have a cushion under their knees, which I particularly recommend for those of us with back problems.

3. Cover yourself with a blanket.

4. Place a soft eye pillow over your eyes. You can also use any soft cloth or a scarf.

Basic Relaxation Pose

1. Lie down on the floor
2. Keep your legs a good distance apart with your toes pointing to the side.
3. Hold your hands away from your body with the palms facing up
4. Rock your head back and forth slightly at first to find the middle point of the back of the head.
5. Wiggle your fingers and toes a little to remind your body to relax.
6. Take a few deep breaths into your belly and allow yourself to breathe out heavily.
7. Enjoy some calming and relaxing music or listen to guided relaxation exercise.

7. I enjoy

Healing bath

Bathtub or hot tub – You may also wish to take advantage of the natural pools. If you're lucky enough to own a bath tub or a Jacuzzi, run the water and fill it with rose petals and rose essential oil. Light some candles and put on some gentle music. Take your time, allow yourself to lie in the bath for as long as you can. Remember to breathe deeply and let the water heal you. Afterwards, apply your favourite body oil or lotion. Enjoy loving your body with every stroke. With your touch, offer yourself gratitude and love. Love each and every cell of you. Leave all negative thoughts outside the bathroom, allow yourself to make peace with your sacred temple, your body, and enjoy a healing moment with yourself.

Shower - For the rest of us who don't own a bathtub, we can just as easily take a healing shower. Scatter rose petals on the shower floor. Light some candles and put on some gentle music. Take your time – stand under the hot shower and imagine that you're standing under a healing waterfall. Feel the water cleanse you. Afterwards, apply your favourite oil or lotion. Enjoy loving your body with every stroke. With your touch, offer yourself gratitude and love. Love each and every cell of you. Leave all negative thoughts outside the bathroom, allow yourself to make peace with your sacred temple, your body, and enjoy a healing moment with yourself.

Your candle light

Choose a nice block candle in whatever colour you feel is most symbolic of yourself. Cleanse the candle with an essential oil. Pour a few drops into your palm, rub your palms together and then apply the oil to the candle. Hold the candle in your hands. Visualize yourself full of strength and light. See the blessing light of the universe surround you and heal you in this moment. Say a little prayer for yourself, either out loud or to yourself. Light the candle and know that whenever this candle is burning, its light is blessing and healing you. Remember to light the candle regularly. You can do this whenever you feel like you are losing your strength— light a candle for yourself and ask your angels or whatever you believe in for protection.

Keep your candle in a favourite place in your home — you may even want to build yourself a healing altar on a shelf, table, or window sill.

With your candle burning, allow yourself to sit comfortably and listen to a guided meditation or calming music.

8. The Goddess

The Goddess has always fascinated me. When I was a little girl, I was certain that God was a woman. Over the years, I've put a lot of time into learning all I can about the Goddesses of the world and all that has been written about them throughout history. Whenever I talk about the Goddess, I mean it in the sense of the Great Spirit. If you want, you can replace the word 'Goddess' with God, the Great Spirit, or whatever suits you and your chosen path. The Goddess is just my way of coming closer to the Light, or the good in the world.

Over the years and throughout everything that's happened in my life, I've sought strength in nature and through my connection with the Goddesses and Mother Earth. Whenever I need inner peace and calm, I look very much towards nature. I love to walk in nature and connect with the tranquility that Mother Earth brings. This is one of the things that has empowered me throughout all the hardship I've experienced in my life.

I conversed with the Goddess on a daily basis during the peak of our IVF process. I meditated a lot and tried my best to form a connection with Her. On my darkest days, I even thought I'd lost my faith — that God, the Goddess, or the Great Spirit simply could not exist when there's so much suffering in life. I remember asking the Goddess every day if She was there and never receiving an answer — only silence. Deep, infinite silence. It was in this silence that I sat, and ultimately felt that the silence was the embrace of the Mother. Throughout it all, I felt Her embrace. I realised that this Mother Energy was so strong that it had in fact ignited my desire to become a mother myself. This maternal energy resides in all of us, both men and women — even woman who can't bear children, and therein lies a beautiful opportunity. An opportunity to connect with the Mother Energy, the gentle Goddess. Because even if we can't make children, we can still create. We can nurture our dreams and offer to the world all that lives within. I believe that everyone is given a task in this life, and that our creations possess an infinite power to heal ourselves and others. Nurturing myself and learning to become a better person with each passing day has brought me peace.

There were nine women who took care of me the day I went into surgery in Copenhagen. Nine women who were either doctors or nurses. All were radiant with the beauty and light of the Goddess. All supporting me with sincerity through this procedure, this rite of passage, this healing.

Once I was back home from the hospital and had begun my healing process, it came to my attention that all of the procedures I'd gone through — a ruptured appendix, laparoscopies, surgeries — had given me nine scars on my abdomen.

The number nine had begun to pique my interest. Why was this number suddenly popping up everywhere at this turning point in my life? I'm curious by nature and all things spiritual captivate my interest. I started contemplating, and felt a sense of awe come over me when I discovered much has been written about the number nine in the spiritual world.

The three faces of the Goddess and the number nine

In Goddess mythology and the study of world spirituality, the number nine is often spoken of as a symbol of wisdom and initiation. It represents spiritual energy and carries a great emotionally transformative force. Many cultures around the world tell stories of the nine fold Goddess, who is in fact the triple Goddess multiplied by three – this eternal road that is our path home.

-Greek mythology speaks of the nine muses or goddesses, each of whom possesses either the power of scientific knowledge, the arts, or literature.

-Celtic mythology speaks of nine sisters, each of whom possesses either a force of nature or the environment.

-In Norse mythology, Rán has nine daughters — goddesses or muses who possess artistic power and energy, and are connected with the energies of the ocean.

-Icelandic folklore refers to nine women. The story of Þiðrandi from Ólafssaga features nine black-clad women who symbolize the old times, and nine white-clad women who symbolize the new. These women are said to be fylgjur, or protective beings or Goddesses.

I believe that during significant times in our lives, the energies we need in order to overcome reveal themselves to us and support us as we learn from the process. I believe that all the surgeries I've had have been a rite of passage or a healing journey for me, and have in fact motivated me to write this.

Throughout this process, the triple goddess appeared to me before, during, and after my operation.

Sometimes in life we need to listen to life itself and its flow to understand the true meaning of it all. I like to see this as a manifestation of life's flow, and how I choose to learn from the process.

In this case, I choose to look at the three manifestations of the Goddess. It is often said in goddess mythology that the goddess and her energy flows in a threefold manifestation of energy. The Goddess appears as the Maiden or Goddess of Love, then as the Mother, and finally as the Crone. This can be applied to a woman's life itself — how each individual life flows from childhood, into adulthood, and then to old age. The same also applies to a woman's menstrual cycle, which follows a certain flow each month. The flow of the Goddess also defines every day here on Earth — sunrise, day, night — as well as the lunar cycle that flows from new moon to full before waning and going dark again.

Learning from life's challenges has helped me greatly — comparing these challenges with the flow that Mother Earth and the Goddess Herself express.

Freyja - The Maiden – The Goddess of Love

The beginning, a fresh breeze, new ideas, courage, fortitude, passion, sense of adventure, taking initiative, sowing seeds, preparation for something much greater, beauty, strength, joy, being carefree, laughter, the feeling of seeing life for the first time, seeing the beauty in the moment, freedom.

Positive manifestation: There's nothing stopping the young woman from daring to make her dreams come true. She plunges ahead with strength and courage. She priorities her own life and work. She dares to do what no others have done, to go her own way, to sow her seeds and show what she's made of. There's a carefree quality and trust about the young woman. Not knowing what isn't allowed and what isn't possible gives her a sense of freedom.

She dares to go her own way and there's nothing stopping her.
That feeling when you get an idea and feel the energy and creativity flow through and around you — it's vital to follow this energy and not to let your thoughts stop you. Anything is possible! Open your arms and feel the wind in your wings. Breathe in the freedom and the power of manifestation. Dreams can and do come true!

Negative manifestation: Society holds back talented young women. It teaches women that they have to look a certain way to achieve success. Young women are taught that they're not pretty enough, they're fat, ugly, etc. Young women are taught to sit and be quiet and not to speak their mind, that their ideas aren't good enough to give voice to, etc.

Frigg – The Mother – The Queen

The compassionate embrace of Mother, creative force, warmth, acceptance, respect, helpfulness, healing, nourishment, compassion, grace, self-confidence, strength.

Positive manifestation: The Mother Energy appears in our life when we learn to take care and treat ourselves with kindness. We learn to nourish our bodies. We respect our body and soul and we gratefully accept the nourishment Mother Earth offers us. We respect ourselves. We choose wisely what we eat and who we surround ourselves with, we mind our health, we respect the life within, we respect our well-being and our happiness.

The Mother Energy also appears in our life as helpfulness and compassion for our fellow human, the woman who is always ready and willing to help and be there for others. Nurses, teachers, doctors, healers, massage therapists — people who work so that others can achieve a better life. Women who give from themselves and are prepared to help everyone and everything to make the world a better place to be. The Mother Energy flows to family, friends, neighbours, and to the Earth itself. The Mother is always present in the enveloping embrace of mothers, grandmothers, and friends. When put to the test, women stand together.

Negative manifestation: The caretaking professions are poorly paid. We often care more for others than we do for ourselves. We don't respect our own bodies and our health. Respect for women isn't a given everywhere in the world. Women speak negatively to and about each other. We women are our own worst enemies.

Hel – The Crone – The Grandmother

Wisdom, stories, legends, and lore. The woman who holds all the stories of the world and of life. Peace, tranquility, spiritual energy. She who brings us closer to our true selves. She who dares to face the shadows, who destroys and rebuilds. Respect, contentment, inner peace.

Positive manifestation: We listen to our inner voice and follow our intuition. We give ourselves permission to listen for advice and answers from within, understanding that we know more and are capable of more than our thoughts tell us. We allow ourselves to find inner peace, to be in the silence and listen. We set aside days to spend in solitude and listen to ourselves, but also to revisit what our mothers and grandmothers have taught us. What do we carry within ourselves that we can pass on to our younger women? We respect our elders.

Negative manifestation: We don't respect our inner voice and intuition. Our society neglects its senior citizens. The youth are placed on a pedestal instead of the elders. We fear aging and believe that old age is ugly and something to be avoided.

I've always been fascinated by the flow of the menstrual cycle and the lunar cycle and how it connects with the magical flow of the Goddess. which I believe is connected to exactly this beautiful flow of the Goddess.

These three women will appear to us at various points throughout our lives. If we just look at one "lunar cycle" in our life, one menstrual cycle, we'll see that this cycle is what every single woman goes through every month. We can then project this onto to every day, every phase, every life.

New moon - New energy - New woman

A time of dreams and wishes, a time to see and to set in motion.

Rebirth – After our period, we're as fresh as a young woman again. We barely even feel our bodies. We're filled with energy and it's nice to just exist, to feel the relief when the cramps disappear and we can do anything. We're fresh and in good spirits. We're bursting with ideas and ready to make things happen.

This is a time for high-energy exercise and other things that bring energy into our life, a time to dance and to have fun.

Full moon – Taking action- Birth

Time to see your dreams come true and your projects become a reality

Around the middle of the month, we start to feel our bodies more. Fertility is at its peak. We feel a need to pamper ourselves and pay close attention to what we put into our bodies. We feel magical things within, and we understand that we are our own creators. We create for ourselves the life that we want to live, and we respect the process. We dare to watch our ideas grow and our dreams become reality. We allow our "children" –or rather, the things we create – to have a life of their own. We enjoy watching our creations develop and mature, and we respect what we bring into the world.

It is a time for walks and light physical work, for yoga or exercise where we look within ourselves and listen to what our body needs.

Darkness - Peace – Spirituality

Time to look within and see what resides within

At the end of the lunar cycle comes the premenstrual stress, the irritability and anger, until we start to bleed and our body relaxes, releasing the tension that's been building up for the past few weeks. We tend to be achy and to need more rest than we normally do. We're often angry and irritated and we take it out on ourselves and those closest to us — even on our lives in general. This is the time for our inner wild woman to shine. Indeed, we should allow ourselves to get angry and let that energy flow through us. This is the time when showing ourselves the utmost respect is our greatest act of integrity. We give ourselves permission to sleep all day, eat whatever our hearts desires (even if it's "unhealthy"), let our partners spoil us. We allow ourselves to be achy, irritable, unkempt, and to crawl beneath the covers if that's what we want.

This is a time for meditation where we give ourselves a break from our fitness routines and the hustle and bustle of daily life. We allow ourselves to get away from others and find nourishment in solitude. Because what we're really doing is rinsing away the old to make room for the next "cycle" in our life. The more willing you are to cleanse, rest, and release, the better the energy you'll bring into the new cycle.

Every new moon brings a new beginning. The new moon gives us the opportunity to listen to the voice of the universe and the Goddess. Lunar energy influences the tides on Mother Earth and also has a profound effect on women, on our monthly cycles and emotions. By looking at the flow of the moon, we learn to better listen to our bodies and our emotions. Once we feel this deep connection between Moon and Woman, we move closer to our intuition and wisdom. Grandmother Moon has followed you all along your life's journey. She holds the enchanting connection between our own inner self and the Goddess. Allow yourself to listen to Her enchanting melody and sense that your own inner song is in sync with Hers.

Following the flow of the moon and the seasons of Mother Earth has brought me closer to my own inner flow. Watching how the body flows in sync with the moon and with nature has opened my eyes even more to the Pearl Mother's beauty.

The Goddess appears in my life

Normally, our projects in life and all that we commit ourselves to flows from birth towards death. But what took me by surprise about my experience in Copenhagen is that I flowed from death towards birth.

Hel – visited me on my way to the hospital for surgery. We'd gone to visit friends outside the city, stayed the night, and planned to take the morning train back into town to get to my doctor's appointment. When my husband and I got to the station to catch the train to the hospital, we saw that train service in a certain area was suspended. We stood there like castaways, not knowing what to do. I had an appointment to see the doctor and it looked like there was no way I'd be able to make it on time. We stood there on the platform surrounded by people in the same predicament, unable to get anywhere. Chaos broke out, everyone was trying to find a way out. As we stood there in desperation, a car came driving towards the platform and out stepped a woman. She approached me and asked, "do you need to get to Copenhagen?" I said yes and she replied, "you can get a ride with me, I'm driving to another platform where the trains are running, you're welcome to come along". She said she had just headed off but when she saw us, she decided to offer us a ride. We were amazed — there were over 50 people on the platform that morning and she'd noticed us. I thanked her profusely since I was on the way to the doctor, and if she hadn't stopped I'd have missed my operation.

I sat up front with her and we got to chatting. I noticed that she had an owl feather hanging from her rear view mirror and told her that I was very fond of owls, they were my spirit animal. The woman replied, "well, maybe it was actually the owl who led me to you on the platform just now!" I asked the woman her name as we got out of the car after the ride, and she told me her name was Hella. A shiver ran through me when I realized that the Wise Woman herself, Hel, had accompanied me that day on my way to my initiation — my operation.

Frigg – protected me during the operation itself. During my surgery in Copenhagen, I felt the great and powerful Goddess wrap me in her arms. Her head rested against the back of mine and she wrapped me in her protective wings. Her wings wrapped around my body and the operating table. Birdlike beings flew from her wings into the doctors surrounding me. The Goddess filled them with a healing energy that helped with the operation, transforming the doctors and nurses into the Goddess herself.

As I began to emerge from the anesthesia, I saw the world in a new light. Tears streamed ceaselessly down my cheeks and all I could do was repeat the word "mother". I'd gained a new purpose. Of course, I was still heavily medicated after the procedure, but that doesn't detract from the significance of the experience.

Freyja – the Goddess of Love guided me out of the hospital that day. When I finally got permission to go home after my surgery, my husband, Jón Tryggvi, supported me as we walked down a long corridor. I noticed a sign in the middle of the corridor marked with the words 'Chapel of Mary Magdalene'. I asked if we could stop in, it sounded like a beautiful way to bring all of this to a close. It was just a little hospital chapel, but with divinely beautiful window artwork by the altarpiece depicting a vulva in all the colours of the rainbow. I sat down and wept. The Goddess of Love was going to escort me out of my initiation— in all the colours of the rainbow. I felt the Goddess say to me, "now you have gained new life".

As we continued down the corridor to the lobby, a veiled woman sat on a chair and watched us leave. A warmth filled me, certain that the Goddess had protected me and helped me throughout this difficult life experience. I know that I had work to do. I felt compelled to write about my experience and share it with the world.

I encourage you to think about your own flow. How do you feel in the spring? In the summer? Autumn? Winter? How do you feel when the moon is full? How is your menstrual cycle? Do your periods usually start on the new moon or the full?

Looking at my flow has brought me courage and a deeper love for my body and my life. It has brought me closer to knowing the energy of the Pearl Mother and my own creative flow. Now I can create my pearls with a deeper respect and be more true to myself in my life and my work.

Each and every one of us carries unique energy. There is nobody exactly like you. And so I encourage all human beings to show humility and respect to themselves and the enchanting flow that life gives us.

9. Gratitude

I am grateful for everything that's happened in my life.

I am grateful for all the difficulties I have endured.

I am grateful for having overcome those difficulties.

I am grateful for sometimes having days when I cry over the fact that I am unable to have children.

I am grateful for the other days when I love the freedom of being child-free.

I am grateful for this deep wound and for having done my best to heal it. I am grateful for finally having put these words to paper.

I am grateful for myself, my strength, my courage.

I am grateful for my sorrow, fear, and hurt.

I am grateful for my consciousness and unconsciousness.

I am grateful for my breath and for being able to breathe.

I am grateful for life.

I am grateful.

Today I am grateful.

Cultivating your gratitude can be a great challenge. I call it a challenge because when we experience all the emotions that come with not being able to have children, there's so much we have to endure before we can find gratitude and make peace with our circumstances. As I've said before, we may never fully come to terms with our situation. But I make an effort every day to pat myself on the back, praise myself, and celebrate my victories and defeats. Because all the difficulty we experience in life not only makes us stronger, but it makes us into the people we are today.

In the beginning, I talked about how this must have been written in the stars before I was born. I often find it easier to think of it this way, because then I don't have to blame myself as much. I try every day to love my body just a little bit more than the day before, to find reconciliation and inner peace, and to face life in love and harmony.

Just the fact that you're reading this may be a step towards reconciliation and peace. Just knowing you're not alone. There are two of us, at any rate, if not more, and my dream is for us child-free women to stand together and experience sisterhood among us. We're all in the same boat and we understand each other's wounds very well. Allow yourself to surrender and see that life is brimming with opportunities to create and to love. Our victories and the works of creation that we bring into the world in peace and harmony are our children.

And I offer you this creation, my dear sister.
May we rise up in strength and find our harmony once more.

I am grateful for you!

Unnur Arndísar

Afterword

I was always certain that I'd take this "secret" of mine to the grave. I never had any intention of talking about it out loud, and would never have written The Pearl Mother were it not for the encouragement and support of Jón Tryggvi, Mom, my family, and my friends. But meeting other Pearl Mothers and understanding the importance of healing this wound by sharing with the world sparked an amazing energy in me and my environment. Humility and vulnerability have brought me endless blessings, and I know now firsthand that our wounds are often the most powerful teacher.

Many thanks go to: Þórey for the encouragement and support and for reading over my work; Ásta Jakobs for her honesty and strength; my dear Rúna for listening from the heart and giving advice from there as well; Guðrún Bergmann for being an endless encouragement — always; Ateeka for the support and love; Kelsey Hopkins for helping the Pearl Mother being received in English; Bylgja for reflecting the truth and being a true friend; Jyoti for being the Goddess incarnate and for seeing me with eyes of love; Gugga for sharing the same wound and allowing me to see this path with eyes of joy; Fríða Rós for always being there; Heather for being my mirror and helping me giving the Pearl Mother an image, so the world could see her beauty.
A thousand, thousand thanks to my dear Mom for the endless support, for going through this all with me, and for loving me no matter what. Thank you, Sverrir, for crying, laughing, and healing with me. Thanks to Andrés and Sóla for listening and always giving the best advice. Thank you, Dad, for helping me smile through the tears. Endless gratitude goes to my husband Jón Tryggvi, my warrior, protector, and companion on life's

journey. Thank you for being my earth, for looking after me and supporting me — always. We walked through this dark valley together, and I never would have survived without you.

Last but not least, I am eternally grateful to all the Pearl Mothers I've met along this journey. You give me the courage to bring my wound into the world.

All this I do for the healing and blessing of the world.

Even though I do not recite my teachers word by word in this book, they have been my source of wisdom on my lives journey, and therefor in everything I do.
I feel it is my duty to respect my teachers - and with a humble heart I give thanks to all of you for being my support & inspiration.

Louisa Putnam
Reynir Katrínarson
Kristbjörg Elín Kristmundsdóttir
Ateeka
Marjorie de Muynck
Kathy Jones
Michelle Kaminski
Stefanía Ólafsdóttir
and of course my lives truest teacher - Arndís Sveina Jósefsdóttir

About The Author

Unnur Arndísardóttir, yoga teacher, musician, and völva, was raised in a spiritual environment. Her mother Arndís Sveina, a massage therapist and healer, taught her to believe in herself and Mother Earth.
With passion and love in her heart, Unnur has traveled all over the world studying various traditions and spiritual paths, all of which have led her back home to Iceland, where she has found a great connection to the energy and beings of Icelandic nature. She has dedicated her life to the Goddess and Mother Earth.

Unnur studied music in Santa Fe, New Mexico between 2003 and 2006. She was fortunate enough to become acquainted with the traditions and philosophies of the Native American, who taught her various sacred ceremonies and ways of healing.

Unnur has been practicing yoga since 1993 and graduated as a yoga teacher from Kristbjörg's Yoga and Flower Essence School 2010. She has worked as a yoga and meditation teacher ever since. She teaches a gentle combination of hatha and raja yoga that focuses on meditation in motion, breathing, and relaxation. Unnur places a special emphasis on inner peace and tranquility in her teaching.
Unnur also studied yoga therapy at the Transformational Hatha Yoga School in Greece in 2016 and Restorative Yoga from Ateekas Yoga Somatics in 2018.

Unnur carries the title Sister of Avalon from Kathy Jones's Goddess School in Glastonbury, England, where she swore an oath to the Goddess and her ceremonies.
Unnur studied sound healing in New Mexico, USA under Marjorie de Muynck in 2008, and also learned about Flower Essences, their power, and healing with Stefanía Ólafsdóttir at Nýjaland in 2011.

In Iceland, Uni retrieved ancient wisdom from the Norse Mythology, through her close collaboration with Animistic Reynir Katrínar. Based on Reynis wisdom, they together evoked the energies of the Goddesses, Gods and beings of Iceland.

Uni released the solo album Enchanted in 2009, and in 2013 she released the duet album Morning Rain with her husband Jón Tryggvi. Together they form the duo UniJon.
Uni was also a part of the duo Seiðlæti with Reynir Katrínar, they released an album 2017 called Þagnarþulur that is dedicated to Frigg and the Goddesses of Fensalir.

Unnur has developed Icelandic earth ceremonies in connection to the Norse Wheel of the Year, where she turns our eyes to the Goddess and her manifestations in Mother Earth all around us.
She also publishes Goddess ceremonies online every new moon and in every season of Mother Earth. There you can enjoy meditation and enchanting ceremonies in connection to the flow of the moon and the earth.

Unnur is infertile but has taken the title of Pearl Mother in an effort to transform the energy around and perception of infertility. Unnur encourages other infertile and child-free women take up the title with pride, and to prove to the world that women without children have an important and healing role to play here on Mother Earth.

Unnur has dedicated her life to Mother Earth, the Divine Feminine and to the peaceful energies of living gently.

www.uni.is

Printed in Great Britain
by Amazon